A Selection from
Your 100 Best HYMNS

Macdonald

Editorial Manager
Chester Fisher
Editor
Bridget Daly
Designers
Camron
Consultant
Peter Max-Wilson
Picture Research
Jenny de Gex
Production
Penny Kitchenham
Made and printed by
Purnell & Sons Ltd
Paulton
© Macdonald Educational 1980
Text © Trident Television 1980

First published 1980
Macdonald Educational Ltd
Holywell House
Worship Street
London EC2A 2EN

ISBN 0 356 07050 6

Hymns have always played a special part in my life. I was a choir boy from the age of seven, and I remember with great affection singing the old stirring tunes in St Thomas Church, Swansea, not always *in* tune but with tremendous enthusiasm.

I also have memories of standing on the deck of the *Stratheden* during the North African landings, leading the Welsh Artillery regiment, to which I belonged, in a heartfelt rendering of *Abide With Me*. It seemed to work, too. We all got ashore in one piece.

Since then, apart from making several L.P.s of hymns, I have had the pleasure of performing many of them on *Stars on Sunday* under the direction of Peter Max-Wilson.

A hymn is a statement of faith set to music and when the right words and the right tune get together there is no finer sound in the world.

Harry Secombe
September, 1979.

CONTENTS

INTRODUCTION

Martin Luther (1483–1546).

The first historical reference to hymn singing in the Christian church appears in the gospels of both St Matthew and St Mark. It was the hymn sung by Christ and his apostles at the Last Supper. Probably it was the group of psalms known as Hallel, which were used at all great festivals during the time of the Second Temple, and would certainly have been appropriate to the feast of the Passover. St Paul refers to the singing of hymns in some of his Epistles which shows that the singing of hymns and psalms played an important part in worship in the early Christian church.

The oldest hymn still surviving to this day is *O Gladsome Light*. We do not know who wrote the original version but it was in Greek and was sung at lamplighting ceremonies around the year AD 200. What it establishes is that Christian hymn singing began in the Eastern Church, for it is not until the year AD 360 that the Christian prelate of Poitiers composed a book of lyrics for singing. Soon after this date St Augustine wrote of St Ambrose, Bishop of Milan, 'He has instituted the singing of hymns and psalms after the manner of the Eastern church.' St Ambrose composed some hymns himself, but there are only three which can definitely be attributed to him, being mentioned by St Augustine, one of which is *God the Creator of all*. Up to the year 1000 many Latin hymns were written, most of them inspired by the reforms of Pope Gregory I who died in 604.

The music for these early hymns was plainsong, whose origins lie in the music of the Jewish synagogue and the Greek modal system. In simple terms, it was rather like using just the white notes on the piano. At the end of the fourth century, St Ambrose fixed on four scales. The great revolution in musical terms came two hundred years later when Pope Gregory added another four scales, or modes, giving us the eight scale Gregorian Chant which is still used as plainsong in the church today. In the early ninth century the Emperor Charlemagne was so interested in music that he invited singers from Rome to his court at Aix-la-Chapelle and founded a school of song which he personally supervised.

Except for the earliest years of Christianity, when the Christians were a persecuted minority, it was not until the sixteenth century that the members of the congregation were allowed to take part in the singing. Until then the singing had been done by the monks, priests or choirs. It is in Germany that we first come across hymns composed and written for singing by the congregation. Martin Luther, who lived from 1483–1546, was the main figure behind the movement to include the layman in the central act of worship, although it was John Huss in Bohemia, nearly a century earlier, who had first written hymns in the mother tongue which could be read and understood by all members of the church. Two books of his hymns, one containing 89 and the other 400, were published by his followers in 1501 and 1505—almost ninety years after his death. Martin Luther's first hymn book was published in 1524 at Wittenberg. It contained only eight hymns, of which Luther had probably written four. He was a musician in his own right, so wrote both the words and the music. Luther can also be credited with introducing more melodic tunes to hymn singing, for it was he who first conceived the idea of adapting popular tunes to accompany his hymns. The lyrics were also written in a similar pattern to those of secular songs. Germany could be said to be the birthplace of the hymn as we know it today, and yet by the 1670s the best output of the country was already past, with the exception of Johann Sebastian Bach. The great period of German hymnody was 1524–1676, beginning with writers such as Martin Luther and J. Walther and ending with Martin Rinkart and Paul Gerhadt. It was Rinkart who wrote that great hymn of thanks *Now thank we all our God* with the tune *Nun Danket* being written by J. Cruger.

In England hymns as such were not yet composed, although there was a source of new music coming into church singing through the introduction of the

English *Psalter* or book of psalms. These new tunes were greatly influenced by the Geneva *Psalter*, which John Calvin initiated during his brief stay in Strasbourg. The final version of the Geneva *Psalter* contained 150 psalms, 110 different metres and 125 tunes, and was published in 1562. For the English congregations the complexities of the psalter proved too great, so a group of common tunes was settled upon and the psalms were sung to these few tunes. Many seventeenth-century poets wrote material which was later used as lyrics for hymns; notable among them was George Herbert with *Teach me my God and King* and *King of Glory, King of Peace*. In 1623 George Wither issued a book of hymns entitled *Hymns and Songs of the Church*, the tunes to which were composed by Orlando Gibbons. However, hymns were not authorised by the Church in England and George Wither found himself involved in legal proceedings. It was some fifty years later that a small collection of communion hymns, by the Baptist Benjamin Keach, was published. The year was 1673. It was to be another 34 years before the first real English hymn book appeared as we would recognise it today. It was called *Hymns and Spiritual Songs* and its author was Isaac Watts, a Congregational minister who is now regarded as the 'father' of the English hymn. Watts published four books of hymns in the years up to 1719. These contained hymns such as *When I survey the wondrous Cross, There is a land of pure delight, Jesus shall reign* and *O God our help in ages past,* which are so familiar today. His greatest contribution to English hymnody was his ability to express wonder, praise and adoration at all the facets of Christian experience.

In the same year that Watts' first hymn book was published, on 18 December 1707, in the small Lincolnshire village of Epworth, a boy was born who during the 81 years of his life was to write almost 9,000 hymns. His name was Charles Wesley and he was the younger brother to John, the founder of the Methodist Church. Their father was the Rector of the tiny parish of Epworth and both boys were to grow up and become ordained Church of England ministers.

The Wesley brothers and the Methodist Movement were to have a marked effect on hymn writing in eighteenth-century England. Their insistence on the inclusion of Christian doctrine and their close following of the Bible for their source of inspiration and sometimes their lyrics, brought a great strength to their work. In Charles Wesley's great Christmas hymn *Hark the Herald Angels Sing* the whole doctrine of the incarnation is contained in these six lines:—

> Veiled in flesh the Godhead see
> Hail the incarnate Deity!
> Pleased as man with man to dwell
> Jesus, our Immanuel . . . .
> Born to raise the sons of earth
> Born to give them second birth . . . .

The simple and direct way he used the words coupled with the beauty of the tune, composed some years later by Felix Mendelssohn, have made it one of the greatest of English hymns.

The Wesleys were also responsible for introducing some of the best of the German tradition of hymns to this country, many of which were translated into English by John Wesley. Despite the Wesleys' firm belief that they had never actually left the Church of England, but had merely spearheaded an evangelical movement within it, it was not until 1820, 29 years after John's death, that hymn singing in the Church of England was authorised. In fact there was a re-examination of church law made that year because of trouble at St Paul's Church in Sheffield, where the Vicar had published a hymn book for use in the church. It is surprising to discover that after nearly 2,000 years of Christianity it is only for the last 160 of them that hymn singing has been allowed in our parish churches.

The outcome of the Sheffield decision opened the gates for hymnody in the Church of England and some great hymns were written. Among them were *Holy, Holy, Holy* written by Bishop Reginald Heber and *Ride on, ride on in majesty* written by Dean Milman and both published in Bishop Heber's book *Hymns, adapted to the Weekly Church Service of the Year* which appeared in 1827. The reign of Queen Victoria was to become the great period in English hymnody. There was admittedly a certain amount of over sentimentalisation in some of the lyric writing

Charles Wesley (1707–88).

and some of the tunes were ponderous and somewhat over written; but when such a vast quantity of material is written in one period of time it cannot hope to be of consistent quality. What was good was excellent, and the appearance of the first edition of *Hymns Ancient and Modern* in 1861 marked the start of the modern period of hymn writing. There were only 273 hymns in that edition as opposed to almost 800 which can be found in the Standard edition bought today. The music editor of that first edition was W. H. Monk who was to have a profound effect on the writing of hymn tunes. One of his best loved was the tune *Eventide* which is associated with Henry Lyte's words of *Abide with me*.

Hymns Ancient and Modern was to hold undisputed sway over the taste of English hymn singing until 1906 when the *English Hymnal* was to make its first appearance. One of the joint editors of this new hymn book was Ralph Vaughan Williams who was responsible for the stirring tune *Sine Nomine* which usually accompanies Bishop W. Walsham How's *For all the Saints*. Vaughan Williams is of course better known as one of the greatest classical composers of the twentieth century. In 1926 the first edition of *Songs of Praise* was

published with a further edition appearing in 1931. Vaughan Williams was again one of the music editors, a function he shared this time with Martin Shaw. One of Shaw's great interests was in finding hymns which were suitable for use in schools. He also did much to revive the use of folk music for hymn tune sources.

The legacy to Christian hymnody from Wales has been the wealth of beautiful tunes which have become famous all over the world, tunes such as *Cwm Rhondda* and *Blaenwaun*. However, there are only a few hymns which have survived translation from Welsh into English; possibly the best known among them being *Guide me, O thou great Jehova* written in 1745 by W. Williams of Pantycelyn.

Since the end of the Second World War there has been an upsurge in modern hymn writing, with the appearance of many 'folk' hymn books, and many of the more forward looking churches are encouraging their use at Sunday services. It is to be hoped that by the end of the twenty-first century people will be able to look back and couple the second half of the twentieth century with the Victorian and Wesleyan eras and say 'those were the greatest periods of English hymnody to date'.

The Last Supper by *Leonardo da Vinci (1452–1519)*.

HYMNS OF
NATURE

Then God said, 'I give you every seed-bearing plant on the face of the whole earth and every tree that has fruit with seed in it.' They will be yours for food.
Genesis, chapter 1, verse 29.

All things bright and beautiful

One of the most famous children's hymns of all time, this was written by Mrs. Cecil Frances Alexander (1818-95). She was born in County Tyrone, Ireland and married the Rev William Alexander, who was to become the Archbishop of Armagh and Primate of all Ireland. She published almost 400 hymns, mostly for children, and the profits from her *Hymns for little children*, which ran to over 100 editions, were devoted to a school for deaf mutes. Equally famous are her Easter and Christmas hymns *There is a green hill far away* and *Once in Royal David's City*.

All things bright and beautiful,
All creatures great and small,
All things wise and wonderful,
The Lord God made them all.

Each little flower that opens,
Each little bird that sings,
He made their glowing colours,
He made their tiny wings.
Refrain

The purple-headed mountain,
The river running by,
The sunset, and the morning
That brightens up the sky.
Refrain

The cold wind in the winter,
The pleasant summer sun,
The ripe fruits in the garden,
He made them every one.
Refrain

He gave us eyes to see them,
And lips that we might tell,
How great is God Almighty,
Who has made all things well.
Refrain

We plough the fields and scatter

The words of this hymn were written by Matthias Claudius. He was a German poet of some standing and lived from 1740-1815. Many of his poems were used for songs by composers such as Beethoven, Schubert and more recently Hindemith. The tune was composed by Johann Schulz (1747-1800) who was born at Luneburg, Germany. He was in the service of some of the great families of Germany and was musical director to the King of Denmark for eight years.

rall. last time

We plough the fields, and scatter
The good seed on the land,
But it is fed and watered
By God's almighty hand;
He sends the snow in winter,
The warmth to swell the grain,
The breezes, and the sunshine,
And soft refreshing rain.

All good gifts around us,
Are sent from heaven above;
Then thank the Lord,
O thank the Lord,
For all His love.

He only is the Maker
Of all things near and far;
He paints the wayside flower,
He lights the evening star;
The winds and waves obey Him,
By Him the birds are fed;
Much more to us, His children,
He gives our daily bread.
Refrain

We thank Thee then, O Father,
For all things bright and good,
The seed-time and the harvest,
Our life, our health, our food;
Accepts the gifts we offer
For all thy love imparts,
And, what Thou most desirest,
Our humble, thankful hearts.
Refrain

All creatures of our God and King

The words of this hymn are attributed to St Francis of Assisi (1182-1226). St Francis was born into a wealthy family of Assisi and at the age of 22 he renounced all worldly riches. Throughout his life he remained a layman but founded one of the most famous orders of Friars. His depiction as a man who loved nature is true but it should not obscure his firmness of purpose in living his life as close to that of Christ's as was possible. Two years before his death, he was marked with the stigmata of the crucified and lived in constant pain.

All creatures of our God and King,
Lift up your voice and with us sing:
Alleluia, Alleluia!
Thou burning sun with golden beam,
Thou silver moon with softer gleam:
O praise Him, O praise Him,
Alleluia, Alleluia, Alleluia!

Thou rushing wind that art so strong,
Ye clouds that sail in heaven along,
O praise Him, Alleluia!
Thou rising morn, in praise rejoice,
Ye lights of evening, find a voice:
Refrain

Thou flowing water, pure and clear,
Make music for thy Lord to hear,
Alleluia, Alleluia!
Thou fire so masterful and bright,
That givest man both warmth and light:
Refrain

Let all things their Creator bless,
And worship Him in humbleness,
O praise Him, Alleluia!
Praise, praise the Father, praise the Son,
And praise the Spirit, Three in One:
Refrain

Spirit of God

Sister Miriam Therese Winter

Spirit of God in the clear running water,
Blowing to greatness the trees on the hill.
Spirit of God in the finger of morning,
Fill the earth, bring it to birth,
And blow where you will,
Blow, blow, blow till
I be but breath of the Spirit blowing in me.

Down in the meadow the willows are moaning,
Sheep in the pasture cannot lie still.
Spirit of God creation is groaning:
Fill the earth, bring it to birth,
And blow where you will,
Blow, blow, blow till
I be but breath of the Spirit blowing in me.

Spirit of God every man's heart is lonely,
Watching and waiting and hungry until.
Spirit of God, man longs that you only:
Fulfill the earth, bring it to birth,
And blow where you will,
Blow, blow, blow till
I be but breath of the Spirit blowing in me.

Think of a world without any flowers

D. Newport

Think of a world without any flowers,
Think of a world without any trees,
Think of a sky without any sunshine,
Think of the air, without any breeze.
We thank You, Lord, for flowers and trees and
sunshine,
We thank You, Lord, and praise Your holy name.

Think of a world without any animals,
Think of a field without any herd,
Think of a stream without any fishes,
Think of a dawn without any bird.
We thank You, Lord, for all Your living
creatures.
We thank You, Lord, and praise Your holy name.

Think of a world without any people,
Think of a street, with no-one living there,
Think of a town without any houses,
No-one to love and nobody to care.
We thank You, Lord, for families and friendships,
We thank You, Lord, and praise Your holy name.

Trust is in the eyes

Estelle White

Trust is in the eyes of a tiny babe
Leaning on his mother's breast.
In the eager beat of a young bird's wings
On the day it leaves the nest.
It is the living Spirit filling the earth,
Bringing to birth a world of love and laughter,
Joy in the light of the Lord.

Hope is in the rain that makes crystal streams
Tumble down a mountain side,
And in every man who repairs his nets,
Waiting for the rising tide.
It is the living Spirit filling the earth,
Bringing to birth a world of love and laughter,
Joy in the light of the Lord.

Love is in the hearts for all those who seek,
Freedom for the human race.
Love is in the touch of the hand that heals,
And the smile that lights a face.
It is the living Spirit filling the earth,
Bringing to birth a world of love and laughter,
Joy in the light of the Lord.

Joy is like the rain

Sister Miriam Therese Winter

I saw the raindrops on my window
Joy is like the rain.
Laughter runs across my pain,
Slips away and comes again.
Joy is like the rain.

I saw clouds upon a mountain,
Joy is like a cloud.
Sometimes silver, sometimes grey.
Always sun not far away,
Joy is like a cloud.

I saw Christ in wind and thunder,
Joy is tried by storm.
Christ asleep within my boat,
Whipped by wind, yet still afloat,
Joy is tried by storm.

I saw raindrops on the river,
Joy is like the rain.
Bit by bit the river grows,
Till all at once it overflows,
Joy is like the rain.

We praise You for the sun

A. M. Pullen

We praise You for the sun,
The golden, shining sun,
That gives us healing, strength and joy,
We praise You for the sun.
We praise You for Your love,
Our friend and Father God,
Who gives us healing, strength and joy,
We praise You for Your love.

We praise You for the rain,
The softly falling rain,
That gives us healing, strength and joy,
We praise You for the rain.
We praise You for Your love,
Our friend and Father God,
Who gives us healing, strength and joy,
We praise You for Your love.

For the beauty of the earth

Folliott Sandford Pierpoint

For the beauty of the earth,
For the beauty of the skies,
For the love which from our birth
Over and around us lies,
Gracious God, to Thee we raise
This our sacrifice of praise.

For the beauty of each hour
Of the day and of the night,
Hill and vale, and tree and flower,
Sun and moon and stars of light:
Gracious God, to Thee we raise
This our sacrifice of praise.

For the joy of ear and eye,
For the heart and mind's delight,
For the mystic harmony
Linking sense to sound and sight:
Gracious God, to Thee we raise
This our sacrifice of praise.

For the joy of human love,
Brother, sister, parent, child,
Friends on earth and friends above,
For all gentle thoughts and mild:
Gracious God, to Thee we raise
This our sacrifice of praise.

For each perfect gift of Thine
To our race so freely given,
Graces human and divine,
Flowers of earth and buds of heaven:
Gracious God, to Thee we raise
This our sacrifice of praise.

HYMNS OF
LOVE

No-one has ever seen God; but if we love each other, God
lives in us and His love is made complete in us.
First Epistle of St John, chapter 4, verse 12.

When I survey the wondrous cross

Isaac Watts (1674-1748) wrote this hymn in 1707 for inclusion in his book of hymns, which was published later that year. In 1715 he wrote the first hymn book for children. It proved so popular that for the next 150 years an edition was issued about every 18 months. Watts is regarded as the 'father' of the English hymn. He wrote over 700 hymns and at least two of them, *When I survey the wondrous cross* and *Jesus shall reign* have remained very popular for over 250 years. The best known tune to *When I survey the wondrous cross* is *Rockingham*. It was composed by Dr Edward Miller who was organist at Doncaster from 1756 until his death on September 12 1807.

rall. last time

When I survey the wondrous cross
On which the Prince of Glory died,
My richest gain I count but loss,
And pour contempt on all my pride.

Forbid it, Lord, that I should boast,
Save in the death of Christ, my God;
All in vain things that charm me most,
I sacrifice them to His blood.

See, from His head, His hands, His feet,
Sorrow and love flow mingled down.
Did e'er such love and sorrow meet,
Or thorns compose so rich a crown?

Were the whole realm of nature mine,
That were an offering far too small;
Love so amazing, so divine,
Demands my soul, my life, my all.

The Lord's my Shepherd

The words to this hymn were originally from the twenty-third psalm, first adapted by William Whittingham (1524-79) and then by Francis Rous (1579-1659) finally revised by the Westminster Assembly of Divines in 1650. There have been many different tunes composed for the twenty-third psalm; but possibly the most famous is that entitled *Crimmond*. Its name derives not from the composer, who was Rev J. S. Irvine, but from the small parish where he was the minister.

The Lord's my Shepherd, I'll not want;
He makes me down to lie
In pastures green; He leadeth me
The quiet waters by.

My soul He doth restore again,
And me to walk doth make
Within the paths of righteousness,
E'en for His own name's sake.

Yea, though I walk in death's dark vale,
Yet will I fear no ill;
For Thou art with me, and Thy rod
And staff me comfort still.

My table Thou hast furnished
In presence of my foes;
My head Thou dost with oil anoint,
And my cup overflows.

Goodness and mercy all my life
Shall surely follow me,
And in God's house for evermore
My dwelling-place shall be.

Jesu, Lover of my soul

Charles Wesley, born 18 December 1707 at Epworth Lincolnshire, where his father was the rector, was the younger brother of John Wesley founder of the Methodist Movement. He was a prolific writer of hymns, leaving at his death, in 1788, no less than 8,900 hymns attributable to him. The most famous tune to this hymn is called *Aberystwyth*. It was composed by Joseph Parry who was born in 1841 at Merthyr Tydfil. He eventually became a professor of music and one of Wales' greatest composers. He died in 1903 aged 62.

Jesu, Lover of my soul,
Let me to Thy bosom fly,
While the nearer waters roll,
While the tempest still is high:
Hide me, O my Saviour, hide,
Till the storm of life be past;
Safe into the haven guide,
O receive my soul at last.

Other refuge have I none,
Hangs my helpless soul on Thee;
Leave, ah! leave me not alone,
Still support and comfort me:
All my trust on Thee is stayed,
All my help from Thee I bring;
Cover my defenceless head
With the shadow of Thy wing.

Thou, O Christ, art all I want,
More than all in Thee I find.
Raise the fallen, cheer the faint,
Heal the sick, and lead the blind:
Just and holy is Thy name,
I am all unrighteousness;
False and full of sin I am,
Thou art full of truth and grace.

Plenteous grace with Thee is found,
Grace to cover all my sin;
Let the healing streams abound,
Make and keep me pure within:
Thou of life the fountain art,
Freely let me take of Thee,
Spring Thou up within my heart,
Rise to all eternity.

Breathe on me, Breath of God

Edwin Hatch

Breathe on me, Breath of God;
Fill me with life anew,
That I may love what Thou dost love
And do what Thou wouldst do.

Breathe on me, Breath of God,
Until my heart is pure,
Until with Thee I will one will,
To do and to endure.

Breathe on me, Breath of God,
Till I am wholly Thine,
Until this earthly part of me
Glows with Thy fire divine.

Breathe on me, Breath of God;
So shall I never die,
But live with Thee the perfect life
Of Thine eternity.

Gentle as silence

Estelle White

All the love of my Lord is the essence,
Of all that I love here on earth.
All the beauty I see He has given to me,
And His giving is gentle as silence.

Every day, every hour, every moment,
Has been blessed by the strength of His love,
At the turn of each tide, He is there at my side,
And His touch is as gentle as silence.

There've been times when I've turned from His presence,
And I've walked other paths, other ways.
But I've called on His name in the dark of my shame,
And His mercy was gentle as silence.

Sing a simple song

Carey Landry

Sing a simple song unto the Lord,
Sing a simple song unto the Lord.
Sing it with your heart, sing it with your soul,
Sing a simple song unto the Lord.
Oh Lord I love You, Oh Lord I see,
Oh Lord I love You, I see that You love me.

Say a simple prayer unto the Lord,
Say a simple prayer unto the Lord.
Say it with your heart, say it with your soul,
Say a simple prayer unto the Lord.
Oh Lord I love You, Oh Lord I see,
Oh Lord I love You, I see that You love me.

Give a simple gift unto the Lord,
Give a simple gift unto the Lord.
Give it with your heart, give it with your soul,
Give a simple gift unto the Lord.
Oh Lord I love You, Oh Lord I see,
Oh Lord I love You, I see that You love me.

Love divine, all loves excelling

Charles Wesley

Love divine, all loves excelling,
Joy of heaven, to earth come down;
Fix in us Thy humble dwelling,
All Thy faithful mercies crown:
Jesu, Thou art all compassion,
Pure, unbounded love Thou art;
Visit us with Thy salvation,
Enter every trembling heart.

Come, almighty to deliver,
Let us all Thy grace receive;
Suddenly return, and never,
Never more Thy temples leave;
Thee we would be always blessing,
Serve Thee as Thy hosts above,
Pray, and praise Thee, without ceasing,
Glory in Thy perfect love.

Finish then Thy new creation,
Pure and spotless let us be;
Let us see Thy great salvation,
Perfectly restored in Thee;
Changed from glory into glory,
Till in heaven we take our place,
Till we cast our crowns before Thee,
Lost in wonder, love and praise.

There is a green hill far away

Cecil Frances Alexander

There is a green hill far away,
Without a city wall,
Where the dear Lord was crucified
Who died to save us all.

We may not know, we cannot tell
What pains He had to bear;
But we believe it was for us
He hung and suffered there.

He died that we might be forgiven,
He died to make us good,
That we might go at last to heaven,
Saved by His precious blood.

There was no other good enough
To pay the price of sin;
He only could unlock the gate
Of heaven, and let us in.

O dearly, dearly has He loved,
And we must love Him too,
And trust in His redeeming blood,
And try His works to do.

One world built on a firm foundation

Geoffrey O'Hara

One world built on a firm foundation,
Built on a firm foundation of peace.
What a wondrous sight,
Freedom's flame alight,
In a world where war shall cease;
One world built on love and peace.

When God smiled, bright sunlight flooded hills and plains,
Song-birds filled green valleys with their glad refrains;
All things God created,
His great love to share,
Now let men and nations
Join and shout it everywhere.

One world built on a firm foundation,
One world no longer cursed by war,
Let no mortal man
Change the Master's plan,
One great world at peace once more.

HYMNS OF
FAITH

Now faith is being sure of what we hope for and certain of
what we do not see.
Epistle to the Hebrews, chapter 11, verse 1.

Abide with me

The author, Henry Francis Lyte, was born in 1793. He was educated at Trinity College, Dublin and took holy orders. For 25 years he was the vicar of Lower Brixham, Devon and is chiefly remembered for his hymn writing. The composer of its famous tune *Eventide* was W. H. Monk, the music editor of *Hymns Ancient and Modern*, who was only 24 at the time.

Abide with me; fast falls the eventide;
The darkness deepens; Lord with me abide;
When other helpers fail, and comforts flee,
Help of the helpless, O abide with me.

Swift to its close ebbs out life's little day;
Earth's joys grow dim, its glories pass away;
Change and decay in all around I see:
O Thou who changest not, abide with me!

I need Thy presence every passing hour;
What but Thy grace can foil the tempter's power?
Who like Thyself my guide and stay can be?
Through cloud and sunshine, Lord abide with me.

I fear no foe, with Thee at hand to bless;
Ills have no weight, and tears no bitterness;
Where is death's sting? Where, grave, Thy victory?
I triumph still, if Thou abide with me.

Hold Thou Thy Cross before my closing eyes,
Shine through the gloom, and point me to the skies;
Heaven's morning breaks, and earth's vain shadows flee:
In life, in death, O Lord, abide with me!

A safe stronghold our God is still

Written by Martin Luther (1483-1546) this hymn made its first appearance in the book containing only seven others which Luther published in 1524 at Wittenberg. Luther was the first Christian theologian to utter the famous statement that the devil should not have all the best tunes, and he lived and died putting his belief into practice. This hymn has also appeared in hymn books under the title of *A mighty fortress is our God.*

A safe stronghold our God is still,
A trusty shield and weapon;
He'll help us clear from all the ill
That hath us now o'ertaken.
The ancient prince of hell
Hath risen with purpose fell;
Strong mail of craft and power
He weareth in this hour;
On earth is not his fellow.

With force of arms we nothing can,
Full soon were we down-ridden;
But for us fights the proper Man,
Whom God Himself hath bidden.
Ask ye: Who is this same?
Christ Jesus is His name,
The Lord Sabaoth's Son;
He, and no other one,
Shall conquer in the battle.

And were this world all devils o'er,
And watching to devour us,
We lay it not to heart so sore;
Not they can overpower us.
And let the prince of ill
Look grim as e'er he will,
He harms us not a whit:
For why? His doom is writ;
A word shall quickly slay him.

God's word, for all their craft and force
One moment will not linger,
But, spite of hell, shall have its course;
'Tis written by His finger.
And though they take our life,
Goods, honour, children, wife,
Yet is their profit small:
These things shall vanish all;
The city of God remaineth.

Amazing Grace!

This hymn was written by a truly remarkable man whose life story reads like a work of fiction. John Newton was born in 1725 and at the age of 11 went to sea as a cabin boy. Before he was 22 he was master of a ship involved in the slave trade; by 25 he had become a firm Christian mainly due to the influence of the Wesleys. He was subsequently ordained and became the rector of Olney in Buckinghamshire where, with William Cowper the poet, he was to produce the Olney hymn book.

Amazing Grace! how sweet the sound!
That saved a wretch like me;
I once was lost, but now am found;
Was blind but now I see.

'Twas Grace that taught my heart to fear,
And Grace my fears relieved;
How precious did that Grace appear
The hour I first believed!

Through many dangers, toils and snares,
I have already come:
'Tis Grace that brought me safe thus far,
And Grace will lead me home.

Yes, when this heart and flesh shall fail,
And mortal life shall cease,
I shall possess within the vail,
A life of joy and peace.

Father, hear the prayer we offer

Love Maria Willis

Father, hear the prayer we offer:
Not for ease that prayer shall be,
But for strength that we may ever
Live our lives courageously.

Not for ever in green pastures
Do we ask our way to be;
But the steep and rugged pathway
May we tread rejoicingly.

Not for ever by still waters
Would we idly rest and stay;
But would smite the living fountains
From the rocks along our way.

Be our strength in hours of weakness,
In our wanderings be our guide;
Through endeavour, failure, danger,
Father, be Thou at our side.

Walk with me, O my Lord

Estelle White

Walk with me, O my Lord
Through the darkest night and brightest day.
Be at my side, O Lord
Hold my hand and guide me on my way.

Sometimes the road seems long, my energy is spent,
Then, Lord, I think of You and I am given strength.
Refrain

Stones often bar my path and there are times I fall,
But You are always there to help me when I call.
Refrain

Just as You calmed the wind and walked upon the sea,
Conquer my living Lord, the storms that threaten me.
Refrain

As once You healed the lame and gave sight to the blind,
Help me when I'm downcast to hold my head up high.
Refrain

Eternal Father

William Whiting

Eternal Father, strong to save,
Whose arm doth bind the restless wave,
Who bidd'st the mighty ocean deep
Its own appointed limits keep:
O hear us when we cry to Thee
For those in peril on the sea!

O Saviour, whose almighty word
The winds and waves submissive heard,
Who walkest on the foaming deep,
And calm amid its rage didst sleep:
O hear us when we cry to Thee
For those in peril on the sea!

O Sacred Spirit who didst brood
Upon the chaos dark and rude,
Who bad'st its angry tumult cease,
And gavest light, and life, and peace:
O hear us when we cry to Thee
For those in peril on the sea!

O Trinity of love and power,
Our brethren shield in danger's hour;
From rock and tempest, fire and foe,
Protect them whereso'er they go;
And ever let there rise to Thee
Glad hymns of praise from land and sea.

O Lamb of God

Charlotte Elliott

Just as I am, without one plea
But that Thy blood was shed for me,
And that Thou bidd'st me come to Thee,
O Lamb of God, I come!

Just as I am, and waiting not
To rid my soul of one dark blot,
To Thee, whose blood can cleanse each spot,
O Lamb of God, I come!

Just as I am, though tossed about
With many a conflict, many a doubt,
Fighting and fears within, without,
O Lamb of God, I come!

Just as I am, poor, wretched, blind;
Sight, riches, healing of the mind,
Yea, all I need, in Thee to find,
O Lamb of God, I come!

Just as I am, Thou wilt receive,
Wilt welcome, pardon, cleanse, relieve;
Because Thy promise I believe,
O Lamb of God, I come!

Just as I am — Thy love unknown
Has broken every barrier down —
Now to be Thine, yea, Thine alone,
O Lamb of God, I come!

Just as I am, of that free love
The breadth, length, depth, and height to prove,
Here for a season, then above,
O Lamb of God, I come!

Jesus, Friend of little children

Walter John Mathams

Jesus, Friend of little children,
Be a Friend to me;
Take my hand and ever keep me
Close to Thee.

Teach me how to grow in goodness
Daily as I grow;
Thou hast been a child and surely
Thou dost know.

Step by step, O lead me onward,
Upward into youth;
Wiser, stronger, still becoming
In Thy truth.

Never leave me nor forsake me,
Ever be my Friend,
For I need Thee from life's dawning
To its end.

Lift thine eyes

Psalm 121

Lift thine eyes, O lift thine eyes to the mountains,
Whence cometh, whence cometh, whence cometh help.
Thy help cometh, Thy help cometh from the Lord,
The maker of heaven and earth.
He hath said, thy foot shall not be moved:
Thy keeper will never slumber,
Thy keeper will never slumber,
Never, will never slumber, will never slumber.
Lift thine eyes, O lift thine eyes to the mountains,
Whence cometh, whence cometh, whence cometh, help,
Whence cometh, whence cometh, whence cometh help.

HYMNS OF
GLORY

Whoever acknowledges Me before men, I will also
acknowledge him before My Father.
St Matthew, chapter 10, verse 32.

Onward! Christian soldiers

Onward Christian Soldiers was written by the Rev Sabine Baring-Gould (1834-1924) who was born into a well-known Devonshire family. He was best known during his lifetime for the many books he wrote, both theological and fictional, and for his championing of the English Folk Movement. The tune was written by Sir Arthur Sullivan, well remembered as the musical partner of the Gilbert and Sullivan team. He was also a popular classical composer of his day and was the first Principal of the National Training College, afterwards the Royal College of Music.

The repeats may include the introduction if desired.

Onward! Christian soldiers,
Marching as to war,
With the Cross of Jesus
Going on before.
Christ, the royal Master,
Leads against the foe;
Forward into battle,
See! His banners go.
Refrain

At the sign of triumph
Satan's host doth flee;
On then, Christian soldiers,
On to victory!
Hell's foundations quiver
At the shout of praise;
Brothers, lift your voices,
Loud your anthems raise.
Refrain

Like a mighty army
Moves the Church of God;
Brothers, we are treading
Where the saints have trod.
We are not divided,
All one body we,
One in hope, in doctrine,
One in charity.
Refrain

Crowns and thrones may perish.
Kingdoms rise and wane,
But the Church of Jesus
Constant will remain.
Gates of hell can never
'Gainst that Church prevail;
We have Christ's own promise
And that cannot fail.
Refrain

Onward then, ye people!
Join our happy throng;
Blend with ours your voices
In the triumph song:
Glory, laud, and honour
Unto Christ the King!
This through countless ages
Men and angels sing.
Refrain

Tell me the old, old story

The words to this hymn come from a poem, 50 verses long, written by Catherine Hankey (1834-1911) the daughter of a banker. In her early teens she was a teacher in a school at Croydon and at 18 started a Bible class for shop assistants. The tune was composed by William Doane (1832-1915) an American business man who had a great interest in music and evangalism. He never became a professional musician but did work with Ira Sankey on his book of sacred songs.

Refrain

Tell me the old, old story
Of unseen things above,
Of Jesus and His glory,
Of Jesus and His love.
Tell me the story simply,
As to a little child;
For I am weak, and weary,
And helpless, and defiled.
Tell me the old, old story,
Of Jesus and His love.

Tell me the story softly,
With earnest tones and grave;
Remember, I'm the sinner
Whom Jesus came to save.
Tell me the story always,
If you would really be
In any time of trouble
A comforter to me.
Refrain

Tell me the same old story
When you have cause to fear
That this world's empty glory
Is costing me too dear.
Yes, and, when that world's glory
Shall dawn upon my soul,
Tell me the old, old story —
Christ Jesus makes thee whole!
Refrain

How beauteous are their feet

Isaac Watts

How beauteous are their feet
Who stand on Zion's hill,
Who bring salvation in their tongues,
And words of peace reveal!

How cheering is their voice,
How sweet the tidings are!
Zion, behold thy Saviour King;
He reigns and triumphs here.

How blessed are our ears
That hear this joyful sound,
Which kings and prophets waited for,
And sought, but never found.

How blessed are our eyes
That see this heavenly light,
Prophets and kings desired long,
But died without the sight.

The watchmen join their voice,
And tuneful notes employ;
Jerusalem breaks forth in songs,
And deserts learn the joy.

The Lord makes bare His arm
Through all the earth abroad:
Let all the nations now behold
Their Saviour and their God.

O for a thousand tongues to sing

Charles Wesley

O for a thousand tongues to sing
My great Redeemer's praise,
The glories of my God and King,
The triumphs of His grace!

My gracious Master and my God,
Assist me to proclaim,
To spread through all the earth abroad
The honours of Thy name.

Jesus! the name that charms our fears,
That bids our sorrows cease;
'Tis music in the sinner's ears,
'Tis life, and health, and peace.

He speaks, and, listening to His voice,
New life the dead receive,
The mournful, broken hearts rejoice,
The humble poor believe.

He breaks the power of cancelled sin,
He sets the prisoner free;
His blood can make the foulest clean,
His blood availed for me.

See all your sins on Jesus laid:
The Lamb of God was slain,
His soul was once an offering made
For every soul of man.

Lord, Jesus Christ

Patrick Appleford

Lord, Jesus Christ, you have come to us,
You are one with us, Mary's Son.
Cleansing our souls from all their sin,
Pouring Your love and goodness in,
Jesus our love for You we sing,
Living Lord.

Lord, Jesus Christ, now and ev'ry day
Teach us how to pray, Son of God.
You have commanded us to do
This in remembrance, Lord, of you
Into our lives Your pow'r breaks through,
Living Lord.

Lord, Jesus Christ, You have come to us,
Born as one of us, Mary's Son.
Led out to die on Calvary,
Risen from death to set us free,
Living Lord Jesus, help us to see
You are Lord.

Lord, Jesus Christ, I would come to You,
Live my life for You, Son of God.
All your commands I know are true,
Your many gifts will make me new,
Into my life Your pow'r breaks through,
Living Lord.

Mine eyes have seen the glory

Julia Ward Howe

Mine eyes have seen the glory of the coming of the Lord,
He is trampling out the vintage where the grapes of wrath are stored,
He hath loos'd the fateful lighting of his terrible, swift sword,
His truth is marching on.
Glory, Glory, Alleluia!
Glory, Glory, Alleluia!
Glory, Glory, Alleluia!
His truth is marching on.

In the beauty of the lilies Christ was born across the sea,
With a glory in His bosom that transfigures you and me,
As He died to make men holy, let us die to make men free,
While God is marching on.
Refrain

He has sounded forth the trumpet that shall never call retreat,
He is sifting out the hearts of men, before his judgement seat,
O be swift, my soul, to answer Him, Be Jubilant, my feet,
Our God is marching on.
Refrain

Stand up, stand up for Jesus!

George Duffield

Stand up, stand up for Jesus!
Ye soldiers of the Cross;
Lift high His royal banner;
It must not suffer loss.
From victory unto victory
His army shall He lead,
Till every foe is vanquished
And Christ is Lord indeed.

Stand up, stand up for Jesus!
The trumpet-call obey:
Forth to the mighty conflict
In this His glorious day!
Ye that are men, now serve Him
Against unnumbered foes;
Let courage rise with danger,
And strength to strength oppose.

Stand up, stand up for Jesus!
Stand in His strength alone:
The arm of flesh will fail you;
Ye dare not trust your own.
Put on the Christian's armour,
And watching unto prayer,
Where duty calls, or danger,
Be never wanting there.

Stand up, stand up for Jesus!
The strife will not be long;
This day the noise of battle,
The next the victor's song.
To him that overcometh
A crown of life shall be;
He with the King of Glory
Shall reign eternally.

The old rugged cross

George Bennard

On a hill far away stood an old rugged cross,
The emblem of suffr'ing and shame;
And I love that old cross where the dearest and best
For a world of lost sinners was slain.
So I'll cherish the old rugged cross,
Till my trophies at last I lay down;
I will cling to the old rugged cross,
And exchange it some day for a crown.

Oh, the old rugged cross, so despised by the world,
Has a wondrous attraction for me;
For the dear Lamb of God left His glory above
To bear it to dark Calvary.
So I'll cherish the old rugged cross,
Till my trophies at last I lay down;
I will cling to the old rugged cross,
And exchange it some day for a crown.

In the old rugged cross, stained with blood so divine
A wondrous beauty I see;
For 'twas on that old cross Jesus suffered and died
To pardon and sanctify me.
So I'll cherish the old rugged cross,
Till my trophies at last I lay down;
I will cling to the old rugged cross,
And exchange it some day for a crown.

To the old rugged cross I will ever be true,
Its shame and reproach gladly bear;
Then He'll call me some day to my home far away,
Where His glory for ever I'll share.
So I'll cherish the old rugged cross,
Till my trophies at last I lay down;
I will cling to the old rugged cross,
And exchange it some day for a crown.

HYMNS OF
PRAISE

Sing to the Lord a new song; sing to the Lord all the earth.
Sing to the Lord, praise His name; proclaim His salvation
day after day.
Psalm 96, verses 1 and 2.

Morning has broken

This hymn was written for inclusion in the *Songs of Praise* hymn book by Eleanor Farjeon (1881-1965). She was an established poet and author of her day and was asked to write a poem on the theme of thanksgiving for each new day, which fitted the lovely old Gaelic melody arranged by Martin Shaw. The result was *Morning has broken*. Some 30 years after it was written it achieved a worldwide audience as 'pop' record success.

Morning has broken
Like the first morning,
Blackbird has spoken
Like the first bird.
Praise for the singing!
Praise for the morning!
Praise for them, springing
Fresh from the Word!

Sweet the rain's new fall
Sunlit from heaven,
Like the first dewfall
On the first grass.
Praise for the sweetness
Of the wet garden,
Sprung in completeness
Where His feet pass.

Mine is the sunlight!
Mine is the morning
Born of the one light
Eden saw play!
Praise with elation,
Praise every morning,
God's re-creation
Of the new day!

Praise to the Lord

Words written by Joachim Neander (1650-80) who was born at Bremen. He was known as the 'first poet' of the reform church and was for some years headmaster of the Grammar school at Dusseldorf. He returned to Bremen at the age of 29 and worked as assistant preacher at St. Martin's church. He died the following year of consumption having written some 60 hymns in his short life.

The translation into English of this hymn was done by Catherine Winkworth (1827-1878).

Praise to the Lord, the Almighty,
the King of creation;
O my soul, praise Him, for He is thy
health and salvation;
Come ye who hear,
Brothers and sisters draw near,
Praise Him in glad adoration.

Praise to the Lord, who o'er all things
So wondrously reigneth,
Shelters thee under His wings,
Yea, so gently sustaineth
Hast thou not seen?
All that is needful hath been
Granted in what He ordaineth.

Praise to the Lord, who doth prosper
thy work and defend thee;
Surely His goodness and mercy here
daily attend thee:
Ponder anew
All the Almighty can do,
He who with love doth befriend thee.

Praise to the Lord, who, when tempests
their warfare are waging,
Who, when the elements madly
around thee are raging
Biddeth them cease,
Turneth their fury to peace,
Whirlwinds and waters assuaging.

Praise to the Lord, who when darkness
of sin is abounding,
Who, when the godless do triumph,
all virtue confounding,
Sheddeth His light,
Chaseth the horrors of night,
Saints with His mercy surrounding.

Praise to the Lord! O let all that is
in me adore Him!
All that hath life and breath, come now
with praises before Him!
Let the Amen
Sound from His people again:
Gladly for aye we adore Him.

When morning gilds
the skies

Anon

When morning gilds the skies,
My heart awaking cries:
May Jesus Christ be praised!
Alike at work and prayer
To Jesus I repair:
May Jesus Christ be praised!

Where'er the sweet church bell,
Peals over hill and dale,
May Jesus Christ be praised!
Oh hark it! What it sings
As joyously it rings—
May Jesus Christ be praised!

My tongue shall never tire
Of chanting with the choir:
May Jesus Christ be praised!
This song of sacred joy,
It never seems to cloy,
May Jesus Christ be praised!

Does sadness fill my mind?
A solace here I find—
May Jesus Christ be praised!
When evil thoughts molest,
With this I shield my breast—
May Jesus Christ be praised!

Let earth's wide circle round
In joyful notes resound:
May Jesus Christ be praised!
Let air, and sea, and sky,
From depth to height, reply:
May Jesus Christ be praised!

Be this while life is mine,
My canticle divine,
May Jesus Christ be praised!
Be this the eternal song
Through all the ages long,
May Jesus Christ be praised!

All hail the power of
Jesu's name

Edward Perronet

All hail the power of Jesu's name;
Let angels prostrate fall;
Bring forth the royal diadem
To crown Him Lord of all.

Crown Him, ye martyrs of our God,
Who from His altar call;
Extol Him in whose path ye trod,
And crown Him Lord of all.

Ye seed of Israel's chosen race,
Ye ransomed from the fall,
Hail Him who saves you by His grace,
And crown Him Lord of all.

Sinners! whose love can ne'er forget
The wormwood and the gall;
Go spread your trophies at His feet,
And crown Him Lord of all.

Let every tribe and every tongue
Before Him prostrate fall,
And shout in universal song
The crowned Lord of all.

O that with yonder sacred throng
We at His feet may fall,
Join in the everlasting song,
And crown Him Lord of all!

All glory, laud and honour

Theodulf of Orleans

All glory, laud and honour
To Thee, Redeemer, King,
To whom the lips of children
Made sweet hosannas ring!

Thou art the King of Israel
Thou David's royal Son,
Who in the Lord's name comest,
The King and blessed One.
Refrain

The company of angels
Are praising Thee on high,
And mortal men and all things
Created make reply.
Refrain

The people of the Hebrews
With palms before Thee went;
Our praise, and prayer, and anthems
Before Thee we present.
Refrain

To Thee before Thy passion
They sang their hymns of praise;
To Thee now high exalted
Our melody we raise.
Refrain

Thou didst accept their praises;
Accept the prayers we bring,
Who in all good delightest,
Thou good and gracious King.
Refrain

Praise, my soul, the King of heaven

Henry Francis Lyte

Praise, my soul, the King of heaven,
To His feet thy tribute bring;
Ransomed, healed, restored, forgiven,
Who like thee His praise should sing?
Praise Him! Praise Him!
Praise the everlasting King.

Praise Him for His grace and favour
To our fathers in distress;
Praise Him, still the same for ever,
Slow to chide and swift to bless;
Praise Him! Praise Him!
Glorious in His faithfulness.

Father-like, He tends and spares us;
Well our feeble frame He knows;
In His hands He gently bears us,
Rescues us from all our foes:
Praise Him! Praise Him!
Widely as His mercy flows.

Angels in the height, adore Him;
Ye behold Him face to face;
Sun and moon, bow down before Him;
Dwellers all in time and space.
Praise Him! Praise Him!
Praise with us the God of grace.

Let the cosmos ring

Jack Green

Let the cosmos ring as we shout and sing,
For Jesus Christ our King.
Let the cosmos ring as we clap and sing,
For Jesus Christ our King.

Praise Him in the towering buildings,
Praise Him in the dark alleyways.
Praise Him in the wet, windy weather,
Praise Him in the dawn, newly born.

Let the cosmos ring as we shout and sing,
For Jesus Christ our King.
Let the cosmos ring as we clap and sing,
For Jesus Christ our King.

Praise Him with the shouts of the children,
Praise Him with the rumble of trains.
Praise Him in the heat of the sunshine,
Praise Him on the freshly mown lawn.

Let the cosmos ring as we shout and sing,
For Jesus Christ our King.
Let the cosmos ring as we clap and sing,
For Jesus Christ our King.

Praise Him, Praise Him, Praise Him!

All people that on earth do dwell

William Kethe

All people that on earth do dwell,
Sing to the Lord with cheerful voice;
Him serve with mirth, His praise forth tell;
Come ye before Him and rejoice.

The Lord we know is God indeed;
Without our aid He did us make:
We are His folk, He doth us feed;
And for His sheep He doth us take.

O enter then His gates with praise;
Approach with joy His courts unto;
Praise, laud, and bless His name always,
For it is seemly so to do.

For why? The Lord our God is good;
His mercy is for ever sure;
His truth at all times firmly stood,
And shall from age to age endure.

HYMNS OF
THANKSGIVING AND JOY

Shout for joy to the Lord, all the earth. Serve the Lord with gladness; come before him with joyful songs.
Psalm 100, verses 1 and 2.

Now thank we all our God

Written by Martin Rinkart (1586-1649) Precentor of the church at Eisleben (which was Martin Luther's birth place), as a thanksgiving for the end of the Thirty Years war. The tune, *Nun Danket*, is ascribed to Johan Cruger (1598-1662) Cantor of St Nicholas's church in Berlin; although it is more than possible that Rinkart wrote the original melody line himself.

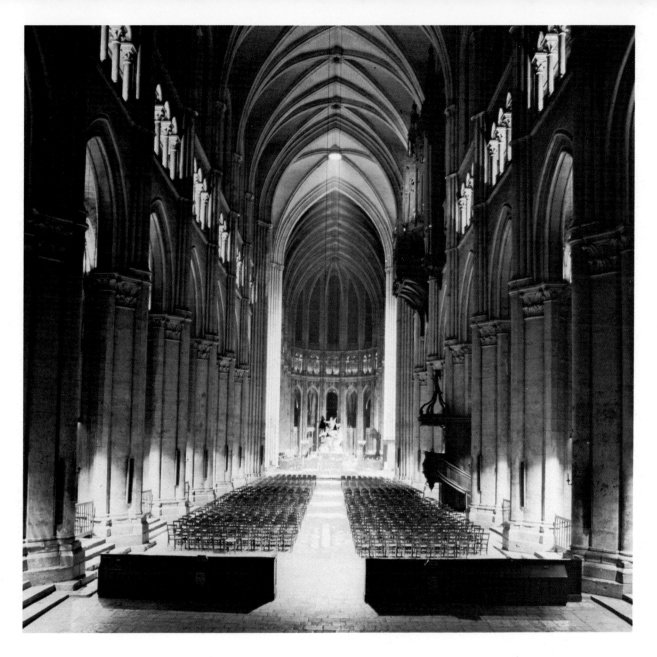

Now thank we all our God,
With hearts, and hands, and voices;
Who wondrous things hath done,
In whom His world rejoices;
Who, from our mothers' arms,
Hath blessed us on our way
With countless gifts of love,
And still is ours to-day.

O may this bounteous God
Through all our life be near us,
With ever-joyful hearts
And blessed peace to cheer us,
And keep us in His grace,
And guide us when perplexed,
And free us from all ills
In this world and the next.

All praise and thanks to God
The Father now be given,
The Son, and Him who reigns
With Them in highest heaven:
The one, eternal God
Whom earth and heaven adore;
For thus it was, is now,
And shall be evermore.

For all the saints

This hymn was written by Bishop William Walsham How (1823-1897) who was the first Bishop of Wakefield when it was made a diocise in 1888. He was for some years Bishop of Bedford and was well known for his work in connection with the poor of the East End of London. The composer of the best-known tune to this hymn, *Sine Nomine*, was Ralph Vaughan Williams who was joint editor of the 1926 and 1931 editions of the *English Hymnal*.

For all the saints who from their labours rest,
Who Thee by faith before the world confessed,
Thy name, O Jesu, be for ever blest.
Alleluia!

[Might;
Thou wast their Rock, their Fortress, and their
Thou, Lord, their Captain in the well fought fight;
Thou in the darkness drear their one true Light.
Alleluia!

O may Thy soldiers, faithful, true and bold,
Fight as the saints who nobly fought of old,
And win, with them, the victor's crown of gold!
Alleluia!

O blest communion, fellowship divine!
We feebly struggle; they in glory shine,
Yet all are one in Thee, for all are Thine.
Alleluia!

And when the strife is fierce, the warfare long,
Steals on the ear the distant triumph song
And hearts are brave again, and arms are strong.
Alleluia!

The golden evening brightens in the west;
Soon, soon to faithful warriors cometh rest;
Sweet is the calm of paradise the blest.
Alleluia!

But lo! there breaks a yet more glorious day:
The saints triumphant rise in bright array;
The King of Glory passes on His way.
Alleluia!

[coast,
From earth's wide bounds, from ocean's farthest
Through gates of pearl streams in the countless
Singing to Father, Son, and Holy Ghost: [host,
Alleluia!

Through the night
Thy angels kept

W. Canton

Through the night Thy angels kept
Watch beside me while I slept ;
Now the dark has passed away,
Thank Thee, Lord, for this new day.

North and south and east and west
May Thy holy name be blest;
Everywhere beneath the sun,
As in heaven Thy will be done.

Through the night Thy angels kept
Watch beside me while I slept ;
Now the dark has passed away,
Thank Thee, Lord, for this new day.

Give me food that I may live;
Every naughtiness forgive;
Keep all evil things away
From Thy little child this day.

Through the night Thy angels kept
Watch beside me while I slept ;
Now the dark has passed away,
Thank Thee, Lord, for this new day.

Jesus shall reign
where'er the sun

Isaac Watts

Jesus shall reign where'er the sun
Doth his successive journeys run;
His kingdom stretch from shore to shore,
Till suns shall rise and set no more.

For Him shall endless prayer be made,
And praises throng to crown His head;
His name like sweet perfume shall rise
With every morning sacrifice.

People and realms of every tongue
Dwell on His love with sweetest song;
And infant voices shall proclaim
Their young hosannas to His name.

Blessings abound where'er He reigns;
The prisoner leaps to lose his chains;
The weary find eternal rest;
And all the sons of want are blest.

Where He displays His healing power,
Death and the curse are known no more;
In Him the tribes of Adam boast
More blessings than their father lost.

Let every creature rise, and bring
Its grateful honours to our King;
Angels descend with songs again,
And earth prolong the joyful strain.

Lift up your hearts

Henry Montagu Butler

Lift up your hearts! We lift them Lord, to Thee;
Here at Thy feet none other may we see;
Lift up your hearts! E'en so, with one accord,
We lift them up, we lift them to the Lord.

Above the level of the former years,
The mire of sin, the slough of guilty fears,
The mist of doubt, the blight of love's decay,
O Lord of Light, lift all our hearts today!

Above the swamps of subterfuge and shame,
The deeds, the thoughts that honour may not name,
The halting tongue that dares not tell the whole,
O Lord of Truth, lift every Christian soul!

Lift every gift that Thyself hast given;
Low lies the best till lifted up to heaven:
Low lie the bounding heart, the teeming brain,
Till, sent from God, they mount to God again.

Then, as the trumpet-call, in after years:
Lift up your hearts, rings pealing in our ears,
Still shall those hearts respond, with full accord:
We lift them up, we lift them to the Lord!

O worship the King

Robert Grant

O worship the King,
All glorious above;
O gratefully sing
His power and His love:
Our Shield and Defender,
The ancient of days,
Pavilioned in splendour,
And girded with praise.

O tell of His might,
O sing of His grace,
Whose robe is the light,
Whose canopy space;
His chariots of wrath
The deep thunder-clouds form,
And dark is His path
On the wings of the storm.

The earth with its store
Of wonders untold,
Almighty! Thy power
Hath founded of old,
Hath stablished it fast
By a changeless decree,
And round it hath cast,
Like a mantle, the sea.

Thy bountiful care
What tongue can recite?
It breathes in the air,
It shines in the light,
It streams from the hills,
It descends to the plain,
And sweetly distils
In the dew and the rain.

Frail children of dust,
And feeble as frail,
In Thee do we trust,
Nor find Thee to fail;
Thy mercies how tender,
How firm to the end,
Our Maker, Defender,
Redeemer, and Friend!

O measureless Might!
Ineffable Love!
While angels delight
To hymn Thee above,
Thy humbler creation,
Though feeble their lays
With true adoration
Shall sing to Thy Praise.

Sweet is the work,
my God, my King

Isaac Watts

Sweet is the work, my God, my King,
To praise Thy name, give thanks, and sing;
To show Thy love by morning light,
And talk of all Thy truth at night.

Sweet is the day of sacred rest,
No mortal cares disturb my breast:
O may my heart in tune be found
Like David's harp of solemn sound!

My heart shall triumph in the Lord,
And bless His works, and bless His word:
Thy works of grace, how bright they shine!
How deep Thy counsels, how divine!

And I shall share a glorious part,
When grace has well refined my heart,
And fresh supplies of joy are shed,
Like holy oil to cheer my head.

Then shall I see, and hear, and know
All I desired and wished below;
And every power find sweet employ
In that eternal world of joy.

The day thou gavest,
Lord, is ended

John Ellerton

The day Thou gavest, Lord, is ended,
The darkness falls at Thy behest;
To Thee our morning hymns ascended,
Thy praise shall sanctify our rest.

We thank Thee that Thy Church unsleeping,
While earth rolls onward into light,
Through all the world her watch is keeping,
And rests not now by day or night.

As o'er each continent and island
The dawn leads on another day,
The voice of prayer is never silent,
Nor dies the strain of praise away.

The sun that bids us rest is waking
Our brethren 'neath the western sky,
And hour by hour fresh lips are making
Thy wondrous doings heard on high.

So be it, Lord; Thy throne shall never,
Like earth's proud empires, pass away;
Thy kingdom stands, and grows for ever,
Till all Thy creatures own Thy sway.

Jerusalem

The artist and poet William Blake wrote the words in 1757. The stirring setting was composed in 1916 by Sir Hubert Parry, director of the Royal College of Music.

Jerusalem

Slow but with animation

Voices in unison *mf*

1. And did those feet in an - cient time Walk up-on Eng-land's moun-tains green? And was the ho - ly Lamb of __ God On Eng-land's plea-sant pas - tures seen? And did the coun - te-nance di - vine Shine forth up - on our cloud-ed hills? And was Je -

poco rit.

-ru – sa-lem build – ed here A-mong those dark sa – tan – ic mills?

2. Bring me my bow of burn-ing

gold! Bring me my ar-rows of de – sire! Bring me my spear! O clouds, un-

-fold! Bring me my cha – ri-ot of fire! I will not cease from men-tal

fight, Nor shall my sword sleep in my hand, Till we have built Je - ru - sa - lem In Eng-land's green and plea-sant land.

Credits

Heather Angel, 9
Clive Barda, 2
British Tourist Authority, Back Cover
City and Manchester Art Galleries, 23
Cooper-Bridgeman Library, 6, 31
Daily Telegraph Colour Library/Helen Cole, Title Page
Daily Telegraph Colour Library/Donnelly, 27
Daily Telegraph Colour Library/Redfern, 53
Daily Telegraph Colour Library/Thurston, 45
Daily Telegraph Colour Library/Westair, 37
Dept. of the Environment, Front Cover
Mary Evans, 4
Susan Griggs Agency/Adam Woolfitt, 7

Sonia Halliday, 55
Alan Harbour, Back Cover
Robert Harding Associates, 47
Robert Harding Associates/Carol Jopp, 29
Camilla Jessel, 17
Mansell, 5
Medici Society, 13, 21
National Gallery, London, 19, 33, 41, 57
Salvation Army Headquarters, 39
Science Museum, London, 61
Tessa Traeger, 49
ZEFA, 11

The music *Sine Nomine* by
Ralph Vaughan Williams (1872–1958)
is reproduced from the *English Hymnal*
by permission of Oxford University Press.